CHILE

CHILE
LAND OF
POETS AND PATRIOTS

DISCOVERING our HERITAGE

By Irene Flum Galvin

DILLON PRESS, INC.
Minneapolis, Minnesota 55415

To Tom, Rachel, and Danny

Acknowledgments

Thanks to Ann Curtis, RSM; Janet Korn, RSM; Sylvia Salaff; Maureen Servas, RSM; my editor, Lisa Erskine; and the many others who helped in the preparation of this book. Special thanks to my Chilean family and friends.

Excerpts from Memoirs *by Pablo Neruda which appear on pages 21 and 31 are reprinted by permission of Farrar, Straus and Giroux, Inc. English translation copyright © 1976, 1977 by Farrar, Straus and Giroux, Inc.*

Photos have been supplied by Ann Curtis, RSM (p. 11, 13, 38, 39, 52, 54, 67, 72, 75): George F. Mobley/National Geographic Society (p. 15, 47): Lan Chile Airlines (p. 21, 26, 61, 97); Carol Wulforst, RSM (p. 28, 89); J. Halber, D. Bryant/D. Donne Bryant (p. 24, 92); Louise Spivack (p. 18); Shirley Hall (p. 23); Joan Harkness Hantz (p. 34); Chile Humanitarian Aid and Taller Sol/International Association Against Torture (p. 46); Joseph Flum (p. 44); Defense for Children-International Chilean Section (p. 79); Maureen Servas, RSM (p. 100); Sernatur (p. 102); Wehrner Krutein (p. 110); and Miguel Sayago (p. 112).

Library of Congress Cataloging-in-Publication Data

Galvin, Irene Flum.
    Chile, land of poets and patriots / by Irene Flum Galvin.
      p.   cm. — (Discovering our heritage)
    Includes bibliographical references.
    Summary: Describes the history, people, politics, heritage, folktales, education, sports, holidays, historic sites, major cities, and other aspects of Chile.
    ISBN 0-87518-421-9 (lib. bdg.)
    1. Chile—Juvenile literature. [1. Chile.]   I. Title.
II. Series.
F3058.5.G35   1990
983—dc20   89-28747
                                                CIP
                                                AC

Dillon Press, Inc., 242 Portland Avenue South
Minneapolis, Minnesota 55415

Printed in the United States of America
1 2 3 4 5 6 7 8 9 10 99 98 97 96 95 94 93 92 91 90

Contents

Fast Facts about Chile

Official Name: *República de Chile* (Republic of Chile)

Capital: Santiago

Location: South America; Chile lies along the western coast of the continent, bordered by Peru to the north, and Bolivia and Argentina to the east; the Pacific Ocean forms the coastline to the west and south; Chile also owns islands in the South Pacific and claims part of Antarctica

Area: 292,058 square miles (756,430 square kilometers); *Greatest distances:* north-south—2,610 miles (4,200 kilometers); east-west—236 miles (380 kilometers); Chile has 3,930 miles (6,327 kilometers) of Pacific Ocean coastline

Elevation: *Highest*—Ojos del Salado, 22,566 feet (6,882 meters) above sea level; *Lowest*—sea level

Population *(Estimated 1988 population)*: 12,748,198; *Distribution*—84 percent of the people live in or near cities; 16 percent live in rural areas; *Density*—41 persons per square mile (16 per square kilometer)

Form of Government: Republic

Important Products: *Agriculture*—fruit, wheat, oats, corn, grapes, rice, barley, rye, beans, cattle; *Manufacturing*—canned goods (fish, vegetables, condensed milk, flour, powdered milk), wool, lumber, wine; *Mining*—copper, iron ore

Basic Unit of Money: Peso

Official Language: Spanish

Major Religions: 80 percent of Chileans are Roman Catholic; Protestants and Jews make up a small part of the population

Flag: Divided in half horizontally, the upper left one-third is a white star on a blue background; the upper right two-thirds is white; the lower half is red

National Anthem: *"Canción Nacional de Chile"* ("Chilean National Anthem")

Major Holidays: New Year's Day—January 1; Easter; Labor Day—May 1; Naval Combat at Iquique—May 21; Independence Day—September 18; Army Day—September 19; Day of the Immaculate Conception—December 8; Christmas—December 25

Peru

Bolivia

Brazil

Iquique

Atacama Desert

Chuquicamata

Paraguay

Antofagasta

CHILE

Andes Mountains

South
Pacific
Ocean

La Serena

Argentina

Viña del Mar
Valparaíso

★ Santiago
Rancagua

South
Atlantic
Ocean

Uruguay

Concepción

Maule
River

Temuco

Bío Bío
River

Valdivia

Puerto
Montt

Lake
Llanquihue

Ancud

Chiloé
Island

NORTH
AMERICA

EUROPE

ASIA

AFRICA

SOUTH
AMERICA

AUSTRALIA

CHILE →

Andes Mountains

Punta
Arenas

Falkland Islands
(Great Britain)

N

Strait of
Magellan

Tierra del Fuego

Cape Horn →

1. Land of the Andes

In the north, hot winds blow across the driest desert in the world. In the south, ancient, extinct volcanoes rise beside clear blue lakes. Throughout the land, the majestic snow-capped Andes Mountains tower over large cities, quiet farms, and vast areas where few people dare to go.

This is the country early settlers called "where the land ends." This is Chile, with its incredible deserts, mountains, valleys, lakes, and glaciers.

Chile is the long, narrow country running down the western side of South America. It is so narrow that it averages only 100 miles (161 kilometers) from east to west, or about half the distance from New York City to Boston. Yet it is so long—2,650 miles (4,267 kilometers)—that if it were possible to lay it across the United States, it would be almost as far as the distance from Miami to Seattle.

Chile is bordered by Peru to the north, and by Bolivia and Argentina to the east. To the west and south, Chile's long coastline lies along the Pacific Ocean, giving the country beautiful beaches and a reputation for fine seafood.

From the hot desert in the north to the icy glaciers

in the south, all of Chile's regions have two things in common: the mountains and the sea. Running like a backbone along the full length of the country, the Andes Mountains tower higher than the Rocky Mountains. People from all over the world come here to ski. Since Chile is south of the equator, it is winter in Chile when it is summer in North America. Skiers who like to train year-round often go to Chile in July and August.

Because of their height, the Andes are used for more than skiing. At Cerro Tololo, 7,544 feet (2,300 meters) up the Andes, astronomers get a close-up view of space. Near La Serena, a town in northern Chile, there are three important international observatories. Astronomers and other scientists come from all over the world to use their large collection of telescopes.

While the Andes are home to few people, they are home to many other kinds of life. The candleholder cactus, named for the way its branches reach up as if they were holding candles, grows high in the mountains. These cacti grow only one-quarter inch (five to seven millimeters) a year and flower for just twenty-four hours once a year. Fog provides just enough moisture for the candleholder cactus to grow.

Even higher up, in Lauca National Park, near the Bolivian border, llamas, vicuñas, and pink flamingos can be found. Lauca National Park is one of sixty-six national parks in Chile.

The Andes Mountains form the backbone of Chile.

The Coastal Range, a small mountain chain, runs along Chile's west coast. Not many of Chile's 12 million people live in either the Andes or the Coastal Range, though. Most live in the central valley lying in between. In their long, narrow land, Chileans can watch the sun come up over the mountains and set over the sea.

The Driest Desert

Chile has five distinct regions. The first, in the north, has the driest desert in the world, the Atacama. There are places in this desert where rain has never fallen. While there is some underground water and a few rivers, people who live here have to get most of their water by piping it over long distances from springs and rivers in the mountains.

People have lived in the Atacama Desert for thousands of years. Huge murals called petroglyphs were created by ancient Indians, and can still be seen on the sides of the Andes. The Indians placed dark stones against the light background of the sand to form pictures of people, animals, and geometric figures. On a mountain near the town of Iquique is one called the Giant of the Atacama. At 400 feet (122 meters) long, or the size of an entire baseball field, it is the largest picture of a person in the world. No one knows what it means

Valle de la luna, *or "Valley of the Moon," in the Atacama Desert.*

or why it was created by these early residents.

The cities in this area grew around the copper, silver, gold, iron, and nitrate mines in the desert. Copper mining, especially, is very important to Chile. It makes up 46 percent of its exports each year. Chile has the greatest reserves of copper in the world, and Chuquicamata, the world's largest open pit copper mine, is in the Atacama Desert.

As important as mining is to Chile's economy,

however, only one in every fifty working people has a job in a mine. Many of Chile's employed people—more than 40 percent—work for the government, either in government agencies, or in one of the many government-owned industries, such as the electric company and the railroad.

The Little North

Between the Atacama Desert and the central valley is a region known as the Little North. This very dry area has been called the "region of 10,000 mines" because it was once a great silver mining region and still has important copper and iron mines. There are long stretches of scrubland, but there are also river valleys along which towns have developed. In the irrigated areas, farmers grow fruit and grains, and raise cattle.

Beautiful Valley

In the middle of the country, from just north of Valparaíso to Concepción, lies a beautiful, fertile valley. The summers in this part of Chile are dry and beautiful. There is rain in the winter, but no snow, except on the peaks of the mountains. The pleasant climate and rich soil combine to make this Chile's most important farm-

The Andes Mountains tower over Santiago, the capital of Chile.

ing region. On large farms, called *fundos*, vegetables and grains are grown, and cattle, sheep, and chickens are raised. Fruit—especially grapes—is an important crop. Chilean fruit is exported to many other countries, and the wine made from the grapes is known all over the world.

Three out of every four Chileans live in the central valley. Most of them live in the country's capital, Santiago. The city stands on a wide plain and is surrounded by the magnificent, snow-covered Andes. On most days, though, it is difficult to see the Andes because of the heavy layer of smog that covers the city.

Santiago is a busy, noisy city of many contrasts. In the downtown area, fancy shops sell clothes, televisions, and videocassette players. When a play or an opera is at one of the many theaters, the streets are crowded with well-dressed people. There are modern high-rise buildings and old colonial buildings alongside noisy farm markets and dozens of modern restaurants. Some parts of Santiago have large, expensive homes. In others, cardboard or tin shacks crowd together along dirt streets. These poor neighborhoods are called *poblaciones* or *callampas* (mushrooms) because, like mushrooms, they grow overnight when people can find no other place to live.

Rising above the streets of the capital are two hills. Santa Lucía, in the center of the city, was once a garbage dump. Trees and shrubs were planted on its slopes, though, and it was made into one of the most beautiful parks in Chile. Today the people of Santiago can walk up through the gardens covering the hill and look across the city from the fortress at the top.

The other hill, San Cristóbal, is just across the Mapocho River from the business district. It is higher than Santa Lucía, and has restaurants, an observatory for looking at the stars, a zoo, and a statue of the Virgin Mary at the top.

In the center of Santiago stands La Moneda, the presidential palace. In 1973, the Chilean armed forces, led by General Augusto Pinochet, bombed the palace and took control of the government. La Moneda has been repaired since the time of this coup d'état, but buildings in the area still have holes in them as a reminder of that day.

Steep Streets and Cable Cars

West of Santiago is Valparaíso, Chile's main port and third largest city. Valparaíso has two very different sections because it is built on hills. The lower section, along the sea, is a thin strip of land with narrow, cobblestone streets twisting among colonial buildings, restaurants, and office buildings. Huge ships from all over the world dock here to take Chilean fruit, copper, and seafood to other countries, and to bring wheat and other goods to Chile.

Right behind these crowded, busy streets rise mountains covered with tattered houses and shacks. The streets going up these hills are so steep in some places that people have to climb incredibly long flights of stairs or take a cable car to go home! With its narrow, steep streets, cable cars, and the smell of salt water in the air, Valparaíso reminds visitors of San Francisco, California.

Viña del Mar is a popular vacation spot for some Chileans.

Just ten minutes by car from Valparaíso is Viña del Mar, a popular seaside resort. Beautiful beaches, palm trees, and flower gardens have given Viña the nickname, "Pearl of the Pacific." Chileans and tourists from all over South America come to Viña to vacation.

Cowboys and Earthquakes

In the central valley's countryside, between Santiago and Concepción, there are many farms. Most of the people who live in the countryside are very poor and do not own the land themselves. Instead, most work for wealthy landowners.

This part of Chile is known for its *huasos*, or cowboys, who are famous for their expert horseback riding. The huaso traditionally wears a poncho and wide-brimmed flat hat as he whistles and races after the cattle during roundup time. Usually he works alone or with a few others on the wide pastures near the mountains. Huasos sometimes show off their skills by competing in large rodeos. The National Rodeo Championship is held in March in Rancagua, fifty-three miles (eighty-five kilometers) south of Santiago.

South of Rancagua, at the end of the central valley, is Concepción, Chile's second largest city. Rolling hills, rows of tall poplar trees, lush forests, and wide rivers surround Concepción. Chileans like to walk up Caracol Hill, which rises above the city to the east. From the top, you can look over the University of Concepción and the low buildings of the city to where the wide Bío Bío River meets the sea.

Most buildings are low here, as they are in much of central Chile, because this is an active earthquake zone. During its 300-year history, Concepción has had to be rebuilt more than once because it was destroyed by earthquakes. It was almost completely destroyed in 1939 and again in 1960, so many buildings in Concepción are new.

Chileans say they know when an earthquake will strike because dogs howl just before it starts. Yet earthquakes still cause great damage. The most recent major earthquake in Chile struck in March 1985. It killed one hundred people and injured thousands more, leaving many homeless.

Lakes, Volcanoes, and Rain

The fourth region in Chile, called the Lake District, stretches between Temuco, which is about one hundred miles (160 kilometers) south of Concepción, and Puerto Montt. Snow-capped, smoking volcanoes, deep blue lakes, and thick forests—all within sight of the Andes Mountains—have given this region the nickname of "South American Switzerland." Tourists from the United

A man sells baskets near Angelmo in the Lake District.

States and Europe, as well as other parts of South America, come to see the beautiful lakes and volcanoes, some still active. Lake Todos los Santos, Lake Llanquihue, and Lake Villarica are especially well known. Chile's national flower, the *copihue*, a red or white bell-shaped flower, is found here.

Pablo Neruda, a Nobel prize-winning poet, grew up in the Lake District. "I was born in a green country with huge, thickly wooded forests," he wrote. "I had a childhood filled with rain and snow...Sometimes it rained for a whole month, for a whole year."

This part of Chile is the home of the Mapuche Indians. Mapuche means "people of the land." The Mapuches were great warriors and were the only native people not defeated when the Spaniards conquered Chile in the 1500s. They lived south of the Bío Bío River, which was considered a frontier similar to the Wild West in the United States.

Over the years, the Mapuches lost much of their land. The government has forced the Mapuches to divide and sell land that for centuries was owned by the community as a whole. Some migrated to large cities. Others, who still own land in the south, struggle to survive by farming. At outdoor markets in Temuco, Mapuches wearing their traditional large silver necklaces and ponchos sell hand-woven blankets, jewelry, and wood-carvings to tourists.

Glaciers and Houses on Stilts

The last region of Chile, the far south, stretches from Puerto Montt to the southernmost tip of South America, Cape Horn. Cape Horn is on Tierra del Fuego, a group of islands owned by both Chile and Argentina which is separated from the mainland by the Strait of Magellan.

This region makes up one-third of Chile, but only 3 percent of the population lives here, because

Mapuche children of southern Chile.

Ancud is an important fishing village on Chiloé.

it rains heavily and is bitterly cold most of the time. There are few roads, just miles and miles of mountains, lakes, grasslands, volcanoes, and glaciers. People who live in the far south fish, farm, or raise sheep.

The condor, Chile's national bird, can be seen here flying high over the Andes. When its wings are spread, they are as wide as three six-foot (1.8-meter)-tall people standing on each other's shoulders.

Southwest of Puerto Montt in the Pacific Ocean is Chiloé, Chile's largest island. Chiloé is home to more than thirty thousand people, most of whom make their living by farming or fishing. In the towns of Ancud and Castro, the houses are very different from anywhere else in Chile. The fishing villages, called *palafitos*, have rows of houses built on stilts over the water. When the tide comes in, the people park their boats under their houses.

Mysterious Islands

Other islands in the Pacific Ocean are also part of Chile. These include the Juan Fernández Islands, where Alexander Selkirk was shipwrecked. His adventures inspired the famous novel, *Robinson Crusoe*, by Daniel Defoe.

Chile also owns Easter Island. It is a small, triangular island with an extinct volcano in each corner. There are hundreds of huge stone statues on the island which have fascinated people since it was discovered by Dutch explorers on Easter Sunday in 1722.

No one knows how the people who lived on this island carved and transported these gigantic stone heads. Some people say they could have used ropes and stones and wooden sleds. Others believe ancient priests must have used magical powers to make the stones walk. Some even say beings from outer space must have helped them!

In addition to the islands in the Pacific, Chile claims a part of Antarctica. Some scientists live there, studying

Giant stone carvings such as these are found on Easter Island.

the wildlife and conducting experiments. They usually don't stay for more than six months at a time, though, because it is so isolated and cold.

Chileans love their long, narrow country with the longest mountain range, the driest desert, and the deepest ocean in the world. "Land's end," someone once called Chile. But for Chileans, Chile is land's beginning—the place they love, the place of their dreams, and the place they long for when they are away.

2. *"If You Go to Chile"*

Chileans are known worldwide for their friendliness. A popular folk song, *"Si Vas para Chile"* ("If You Go to Chile"), says, "The country people will come out to greet you traveler, and you'll see how Chileans love a friend who comes from far away." Most visitors say Chile is a place one never forgets.

People have been coming to Chile for hundreds of years to take advantage of its natural wealth and beauty. Whether they live in a city or in the countryside, north or south, most Chileans share a common heritage. Almost seven out of every ten Chileans are *mestizos*, which means they have both Spanish and Indian ancestors.

When the Spaniards came to Chile in the 1500s, several Indian tribes were already living there. The Atacameño and Diaguita in the north, and the Ona and Yahgan in the south, lost their separate identities when the Spaniards killed many of the men in battle and married the women. The children of the Spanish soldiers and Indian women were called mestizos. Only the Mapuche Indians remained as a separate people.

Since the Spaniards first arrived, people have come to Chile from England, Ireland, Germany, Yugoslavia, and the Middle East. In the late 1800s and early 1900s,

*A Chilean might have black or red hair, brown or blue eyes—
just like these Chilean schoolchildren.*

many British and German people immigrated to Chile
in search of a new life and the opportunity to buy shares
in Chilean industries.

Today, a typical Chilean last name might be Spanish, such as Perez or Donoso, or English or Irish, such
as Edwards or Leigh. Even the founding father of Chile
had an Irish last name! Bernardo O'Higgins, who led

the fight for independence against Spain, was the son of a Spanish mother and an Irish father.

Because of their largely Indian and Spanish heritage, most Chileans have black hair and brown eyes. Many, though, have red hair and freckles, or blonde hair and blue eyes. All Chileans, however, speak Spanish.

Spanish is pronounced differently in Chile than in other Spanish-speaking countries. People in Chile do not pronounce some of the letters in their words. For example, *buenos días* (good morning) is pronounced BWAY-noh THEE-ah, and *cuidado* (be careful) is kwee-THAH-oh. When Chilean children say, "Hi, how are you?" they say *"Hola, ¿que hubo?"* (OH-lah KYOO-boh). When they say "good-bye," they say *"chao"* (chow).

A People of Poets

Chileans like to express themselves and their feelings in many ways. Most Chileans love poetry. They memorize their favorite poems, and even write poetry themselves. Two Chileans became world famous for their poetry after winning the Nobel Prize for literature, an international writing award.

In 1945, Gabriela Mistral became the first South American to win the Nobel Prize. Her real name was Lucila Godoy Alcayaga, but she used a pen name. Mistral was a schoolteacher, and many of her poems are about children. Today, Chilean children memorize these poems and might sing them while they jump rope.

Gabriela Mistral encouraged many children to read and write. One boy who met her when he was twelve years old went on to win the Nobel Prize in 1971. Pablo Neruda wrote two thousand pages of poetry in his life. He is considered to be the greatest poet of the century in the Spanish language. His poems have been translated into almost every language in the world.

Like Gabriela Mistral, Neruda chose to use a pen name. His real name was Neftalí Ricardo Reyes Basualto. He started writing poems when he was ten years old, and published his first poem at the age of fifteen. As a child, he would say, "I'm going out hunting poems." As he grew older, he found inspiration everywhere. He wrote about cats, copper, tomatoes, and even bread. Many of his most popular poems are about love.

Pablo Neruda and Gabriela Mistral also wrote many poems defending poor people and poor countries. They believed that people have a right to a decent life and encouraged Chileans and others never to give up hope.

Some of Chile's leading writers today are Ariel Dorfman, Antonio Skármeta, and Isabel Allende. These writers, among others, left Chile in 1973 when the military took over. They felt threatened by the new government. Nicanor Parra, Chile's most popular modern poet, and José Donoso, a novelist, are among some of the writers who have returned to Chile in recent years. They hope they can change life in Chile through their books and poems.

Many Chileans enjoy going to the theater to see plays performed. Two of Chile's best-known playwrights are Marco Antonio de la Parra and Raúl Zúrita. Plays by de la Parra and Zúrita have been performed in theaters, but other plays have been banned by General Pinochet's government. Dramas or comedies critical of the military government were sometimes censored. Playrights who wanted people to see their plays, though, used actors to perform skits on street corners. A crowd quickly gathered to watch the actors portray a short scene. Then everybody left within five or ten minutes, before government soldiers could come to arrest them.

New Songs, Folk Songs

Many kinds of music are popular in Chile. Radio stations play American rock music, classical music, and traditional folk songs. In the north, the music is influenced by Bolivia. Traditional songs are joyful, played with wind instruments such as the quena or the flute, or with the zampõna, a string instrument. In the south, the music is based on Indian folk music. In central Chile, traditional music has a Spanish beat to it.

Before the 1960s, much of the folk music of Chile had

been forgotten. Then Violeta Parra began writing and playing music which was very traditional. She felt it was time Chileans took pride in their own heritage instead of borrowing music from the United States. This "new" music appealed to many Chileans because it was based on all the different types of folk music heard in Chile.

Musicians such as Angel and Isabela Parra (Violeta's children), Víctor Jara, and groups such as Quilapayún and Inti-Illimani followed Violeta Parra's example. They began playing the quena, a small bamboo flute, and the charango, a string instrument made from an armadillo shell, as well as the guitar and other instruments.

The new songs were about factory workers and copper miners, about washing clothes and walking in the rain. They were about all the people and things that are a part of Chile.

Chileans were saddened when Víctor Jara was killed in the 1973 military coup. His songs are still sung today, and he is remembered as a great folksinger.

Handicrafts of Hope

In addition to expressing themselves through literature and music, Chileans sculpt and paint. Roberto Matta is known around the world as a great surrealistic painter. Other artists make ceramics, weavings, and handicrafts.

One handicraft, called *arpilleras*, was started in 1974.

These arpilleras *show scenes of daily life in a poor neighborhood.*

Arpilleras are wall hangings made by women who sew bits of cloth into the shape of a picture. Each arpillera tells a story about what life is like in Chile. Some are happy scenes—children playing and families sharing a meal. Others are sad—soldiers fighting with people in the streets, or callampas. These kinds of arpilleras cannot be sold openly in Chile, but they are smuggled out of the country and sold elsewhere to let people know what life in Chile today is like.

A Patriotic People

Chileans think and talk a lot about politics, and have since they became an independent country in 1810. They are very loyal to their homeland and proud of its democratic history. At one time, the president of Chile could walk down the streets of Santiago without guards, stopping to shake hands and talk with people.

Although Chileans love their country, they don't always agree on how it should be run. When some Chilean women thought President Allende was doing a poor job of running the country in 1972, they staged a protest. A large group of women marched through the streets to La Moneda, banging pots and pans together all the way.

Since 1973, there have also been many protests against Pinochet and the military government. People demand freedom of speech and of the press. Chileans feel very strongly that it is their right to voice their opinions.

Chilean children, too, are involved in politics. At one time, young people held elections for representatives in their schools. Candidates would announce which political party they supported, and students would vote for the candidate of their choice. While these elections are no longer allowed, schoolchildren show their support or opposition to the government through demonstrations, street paintings, poetry, and music.

The Church's Role

Eight out of every ten people in Chile are Roman Catholic. There are growing numbers of Protestants and Jews, but the Catholic church plays the biggest role in everyday life for most Chileans.

While a large number of Chileans do not attend church on a regular basis, holidays and celebrations are very important. Also, some Chileans depend on churches and other religious organizations for food and clothing. Priests and nuns work with the poor people in the cities, helping them to find jobs, and providing hot lunches. Churches also operate health clinics.

Leaders of the Catholic church in Chile also run human rights organizations. The biggest of these is called the Vicariate of Solidarity. The Vicariate offers safety to people who are afraid they will be arrested, and keeps records of those who are. It also keeps track of how many people have been tortured by the government, and the number of people who have disappeared. Church lawyers help families of political prisoners and those who have disappeared by protesting to the government and collecting information about the missing.

Rich and Poor

Chile is home to the very rich and the very poor.

A young girl paints a sign on a wall asking for "peace and love."

Upper-class homes in Santiago.

Wealthy Chileans might live in high-rise apartments or elegant homes in the cities, and own large estates in the countryside. A growing number of Chileans, however, live in extreme poverty.

Callampas in cities such as Santiago and Valparaíso are home to Chileans who have moved to the city from rural areas in search of jobs and better living conditions. Unfortunately, there are very few jobs for these people. They are forced to find shelter in any way they can.

A población in Santiago.

Some people live in run-down houses, while others live in shacks put together from whatever materials they can find.

On many days, families in poblaciones eat only one meal, and this is from an *olla común,* or community cooking pot. Each family contributes whatever food it can to the olla común, and then everyone shares what is cooked. Even well-to-do people can find it hard to buy certain foods due to the shortages in the country.

In spite of daily hardships, visitors to Chile are still welcome. Most Chileans are eager to see new faces and talk to new people. Strangers in the country know they will be greeted with *"Mi casa es su casa,"* meaning "My house is your house." Through their art, literature, music, politics, and religion, Chileans voice their hope for a better future.

3. A History of Democracy

The first people to live in Chile came on foot from Siberia about ten thousand years ago. They walked over the Bering Strait, which was then dry land, and crossed North America and Central America until they came to Chile. The hunters and fishers who settled in the far south unknowingly gave that part of Chile its present name. Spanish sailors who passed by and saw the fires the Alacalufes had built called the area Tierra del Fuego, or Land of Fire.

In the north, the ancient Indians fished along the coast and farmed along the few river valleys in the Atacama Desert. Archaeologists have named them the *Chinchorros*, or gill netters, since they fished with nets. In 1983, workmen digging a trench discovered the mummies of Chinchorros who had lived 7,800 years ago. They were so well preserved that the bodies still had skin and hair. Archaeologists say these are the oldest mummies in the world, even older than the mummies in Egypt.

For Gold and Glory

Over the last five hundred years, several foreign powers have tried to gain control of the land and people of Chile. In the early 1400s, the Incas of Peru spread their empire south into Chile. They conquered the Indians in the central valley, but were unable to defeat the fierce Mapuche Indians in the south.

The Spaniards were the next to invade Chile. Diego de Almagro led the first band of Spaniards across the desert from Peru. Almagro was disappointed when no gold or silver was found in Chile, and he returned to Peru.

In 1541, Pedro de Valdivia led the next expedition of *conquistadores*, or conquerors, in search of gold, and founded the city of Santiago. Valdivia was known as a very cruel man. When he took prisoners, he sent them back to their tribes with their noses and ears cut off.

The Picunche and Huilliche Indians in central Chile were frightened by the Spaniards' horses and guns and were soon defeated by Valdivia. He later became the governor of Chile, establishing towns as far south as the city named after him. According to one legend, Valdivia was finally killed when Lautaro and Caupolican, two famous Mapuche chiefs, poured molten gold down Valdivia's throat.

The Mapuches, or Araucanos as the Spaniards called them, learned to ride horses and defend their land and way of life. The war between the Mapuches and the Spaniards was so fierce that Chile was called the "Cemetery of the Spaniards." One Spanish soldier was impressed by the bravery of the Mapuches and wrote a poem called "La Araucano." Alonso de Ercilla y Zúñiga's poem is considered Chile's first national poem, and children in school learn to recite parts of it by heart. Not until 1883—after three hundred years of fighting—did the Mapuches recognize the government of Chile.

From Soldiers to Landowners

Before Pedro de Valdivia was killed, he rewarded the officers who had fought with him by giving them land and the Indians who had lived on the land. The Spaniards forced the Indians to grow the crops, take care of the animals, and work in the mines. Many Indians died from the hard working conditions or from diseases the Spaniards had brought. Since the Spaniards also married the Indian women, within fifty years of their arrival, there were more mestizos than either pure Indians or Spaniards in Chile.

The big estates the land was divided into became like small towns. Each estate had a large manor house for the owners of the fundo, a church, and huts for the *inquilinos*, or workers.

For almost three hundred years, the Spanish king ruled Chile from across the ocean. The Spaniards made the laws and told the Chileans they could sell their goods only to Spain and Peru, where the king's representative, or viceroy, lived. By the 1800s, though,

Bernardo O'Higgins, the founding father of Chile.

people in Chile considered themselves Chilean, not Spanish. On September 18, 1810, Chileans formed their own government and went to war with Spain to win their freedom. This date is Chile's Independence Day.

Bernardo O'Higgins, the son of the Viceroy of Peru, led the revolt against Spain. For seven years, the Chileans and the Spaniards fought. In 1817, with the help of José de San Martín, who had just freed Argentina from Spain, Bernardo O'Higgins and his army won the war. Chile became an independent country, and O'Higgins became its first president.

The British had given the Chileans ships and money to help them win their war against Spain. After Chile won its independence, many English people settled in Chile and bought Chilean businesses, especially those in the nitrate industry. Nitrate, which was used as a fertilizer and to make gunpowder, was then Chile's leading export.

In 1879, Chile fought Peru and Bolivia in the War of the Pacific. The three countries were fighting over the nitrate-rich Atacama Desert. Backed by a British-trained navy, Chile won the war and the nitrate fields. For forty years, until artificial nitrates were developed, Chile and the British received great wealth from the nitrate fields.

One unexpected result of the War of the Pacific was its effect on Chilean workers. The soldiers who had worked as inquilinos before the war did not want to return to work for the wealthy landowners. Instead, they moved to cities or into southern Chile. These people became free laborers, and eventually became part of the growing middle class in Chile.

Chile for Chileans

In the late 1880s, a movement arose called "Chile for Chileans." President José Manuel Balmaceda led the fight to have the profit from Chile's national resources remain in Chile, instead of going to the British and the two new foreign powers, the United States and Germany. Wealthy Chilean businesspeople, however, backed by the British, went to war against Balmaceda. Ten thousand Chileans were killed, and Balmaceda was defeated.

After this loss, workers began to protest conditions in the nitrate fields. In 1907, ten thousand nitrate workers in Iquique, along with their wives and children, went into the streets asking for better living conditions and more money. Soldiers shot and killed two thousand people. After that, nitrate workers, copper miners, and other working- and middle-class Chileans started organizing political parties and labor unions to try to make their lives better. A song popular today, the "Cantata Santa María de Iquique," tells what happened in 1907.

World War I and the 1920s were a turning point in Chilean history. Britain and Germany lost control of Chile's economy, and the United States became the most important foreign power in the country. The three largest copper mines, which produced 80 percent of Chile's copper, were owned by American companies. By the 1960s, American corporations controlled the telephone, railway, and electric companies, as well as many banks.

Eduardo Frei, elected president in 1964, started a program called Chileanization. He tried to nationalize, or take over, the copper mines so they would belong to the Chilean people, not to foreign businesspeople. He also started a land reform program which gave land to the inquilinos and broke up large fundos. By the time Frei's term ended in 1970, most Chileans supported the changes he had begun.

In 1970, Dr. Salvador Allende was elected president of Chile. Allende, a former dentist, headed the *Unidad Popular* (UP), or Popular Unity Party. The UP was a group of six different parties representing Chilean working people. When Allende was elected, many Chileans celebrated because they felt they had elected a president who would try to improve their working conditions as well as their day-to-day lives.

One of the first things Allende did was to start a free milk program so children would receive a pint of milk a day. Before that, many families could not afford

Salvador Allende, Chile's president between 1970 and 1973.

milk, which meant many young Chileans developed health problems. Allende also offered free medical and dental care to people living in the countryside.

Allende continued many of Frei's programs. Several large fundos were broken up and given to the workers. The copper mines were nationalized, and many large companies were taken over by the employees.

Many poor and middle-class Chileans were happy with the changes. Others, such as businesspeople and landowners, thought Allende was hurting the economy with his programs. Some of these people left Chile, taking their money with them. There were many demonstrations by Allende's supporters and opponents. Strikes and food shortages became common.

The Coup

On September 11, 1973, there was a coup d'état, or violent overthrow of the government, in Chile. The military bombed La Moneda in downtown Santiago, which is like the White House in the United States, and President Salvador Allende was killed. In the first few weeks after the coup, thirty thousand other people were also killed.

General Augusto Pinochet, a general in the Chilean army, appointed himself president of Chile. He closed the congress, stopped elections, and suspended the constitution. Political parties and labor unions were

Indian Trail Elementary
Media Center

declared illegal. Many books were burned, concentration camps were set up by the military, and many people who had supported Allende's government were arrested, tortured, and killed. More than 2,500 people "disappeared"—they were arrested and never seen again. Many of their families still do not know if they are dead or alive.

In 1978, Pinochet created a new constitution, which called for a gradual return to democracy. This constitution said Pinochet would remain president until 1990, when a new president would be elected.

The CIA in Chile

No one really knows for certain how big a role the U.S. Central Intelligence Agency (CIA) played in Chilean politics. But much of that agency's activity is described in a report by the United States Senate Intelligence Committee called *Covert Action in Chile, 1963-1973*. According to this report, Americans with an interest in Chile, such as the owners of the copper mines, telephone company, and large banks, became alarmed when Allende nationalized their businesses.

The CIA helped these companies by trying to keep Allende from being elected. The U.S. government believed that if Allende was elected, Chile would become a Communist country.

Allende, however, managed to win the election.

After this, the CIA reportedly spent millions of dollars to make things difficult for Allende's government. According to the U.S. Senate report, the agency paid for articles and reports criticizing Allende in the newspapers, on radio, and on television. It gave money to people and organizations who were against Allende, and it paid truckers to strike so there would be shortages of food and other goods. All these actions were meant to weaken Chile's economy so much that the military would then take over and "save" the country.

Officially, the U.S. government denies any involvement in Chilean politics. The complete story of that time may never be known.

Fruit for Foreigners

Pinochet changed the way Chilean businesses were run and land was owned. The large estates that had been broken into small farms were given back to the original owners, or sold to people or companies that could afford to buy them. Businesses that had been taken over by workers were also given back to the owners. Some of the copper mines were returned to American companies.

Taxes on companies owned by foreigners were lowered to attract new businesses to Chile. Land that had been used to grow basic food crops, such as beans and corn, was sold to these new businesses. Today, foreign companies raise grapes and other fruits, and sell them outside of Chile because they can make more money that way. This is one reason there are so many food shortages in Chile.

After 1973, a few Chileans became wealthy. But in poor neighborhoods, which grew rapidly during the 1970s and 1980s, eight out of ten people do not have jobs.

Changing Times

Chile was a democratic country for 150 years before the 1973 coup—longer than any other South American country, and nearly as long as the United States. After the coup, a great many Chileans worked for the return of free speech and democratic elections.

Other Chileans supported General Pinochet. These people, mostly landowners and businesspeople, felt Chile was better off after the coup. They argued that Pinochet was fighting communism, and that if Chileans did not like that, they were being unpatriotic.

Chileans who opposed Pinochet made their feelings known in many ways. They staged protests, demanding to know what had happened to friends and relatives who had disappeared over the years. They fought back when police and soldiers searched homes and arrested people in an *allanamiento*, or neighborhood raid.

Some Chileans joined groups such as the Sebastián

Chileans feel it is their right to express an opinion. Here, thousands gather in Santiago to protest the government of Augusto Pinochet.

Acevedo Movement Against Torture. This group was named after a man whose son and daughter "disappeared." Acevedo asked the military to tell him what had happened to his children, but he got no answer. He grew so frustrated that he set himself on fire and died in front of the cathedral in Concepción to draw attention to the problem of the "disappeared." In memory of this man, the Sebastián Acevedo Movement protested violations of human rights. They met in front of public buildings, such as the biggest library in Santiago, and unrolled banners with messages such as, "In Chile, people are tortured and the TV doesn't report it." The people sang songs and then tried to leave quickly before the police arrived.

A Vote for Democracy

In October 1988, General Pinochet called for an election in which he asked Chileans if they wanted him to stay in office. More than 90 percent of the population of Chile voted, and those who voted "no" won by a large majority. According to the constitution, Pinochet was then required to hold an election, allowing Chileans to elect a new president.

On December 14, 1989, Chileans voted in the first election in sixteen years. Patricio Alwyn, the leader of a group made up of seventeen political parties opposed to Pinochet, won the election with a 55.2 percent majority.

A Chilean man wears a headband reading, "The majority of Chile says NO" at a rally in 1988.

A former senator, Alwyn was elected to a four-year term beginning in March 1990. Congressional representatives opposed to Pinochet were also elected.

Chileans were so excited by Alwyn's victory that they danced and sang in the streets. People hung flags and posters out their windows, church bells rang, and firecrackers went off as Chileans cheered the peaceful end to the military dictatorship.

Many problems remain for the new government. General Pinochet will be commander of the army until 1998, and will remain a senator for life. The constitution, written by Pinochet, says that he can appoint a certain number of senators and congressional representatives. This could make it hard for the new president to pass laws. Laws made by Pinochet in the past say that those responsible for human rights violations cannot be punished, yet Chileans want to see justice for crimes committed by the government. Also, it is estimated that 5 million out of 12 million Chileans live in poverty. It will take a great deal of time for Alwyn's government to change the policies that led to this situation.

It is a time of great change in Chile, and it is also a time of hope. The Chilean people are happy Chile is on the road back to democracy. Their deep love for their country gives them faith that they will succeed in their struggle for peace and justice.

4. *Legends, Sayings, and Spirits*

Chile is a country rich with legends and sayings. Some date back to the time of the early Indians, and some come from the Spanish conquistadores. Many legends and sayings carry similar themes—the Chileans' constant struggle with the mountains and the sea.

La Laguna del Inca

La Laguna del Inca, or "The Lagoon of the Inca," tells the story of a beautiful deep green lagoon near Portillo, in the Andes Mountains.

Before the Spaniards came to Spain, the Incas of Peru had moved southward into Chile. Because the Incas considered themselves children of the sun, they held their religious ceremonies high on the tops of mountains, close to the sun.

According to legend, the Incan prince Illi-Yanqui was going to be married to the princess Kora-Lle. Illi-Yanqui was very much in love with the princess, who had deep, beautiful green eyes and was the loveliest girl in the whole Incan empire.

On the day of the ceremony, the prince and princess went with their families, friends, and attendants to

Mount Aconcagua, the highest peak in the Andes, and gathered near a beautiful lagoon with clear waters.

After the ceremony was finished, the princess had to walk down a steep mountainside, followed by her attendants. The path was narrow and stony, with a steep drop on both sides. It wasn't an easy walk for the princess, who was wearing a long wedding dress decorated with heavy, fabulous jewels.

Suddenly the princess slipped. To everyone's horror, Kora-Lle fell over the cliff, her cries echoing in the mountains. Prince Illi-Yanqui raced down to where she had fallen, but it was too late; the princess was dead. He picked up her body and slowly climbed back up the mountain. He didn't take his eyes off his princess. Somehow, the terrible fall had not bruised her skin and she had a strange, peaceful look on her face.

The prince did not want an ordinary burial for the princess. He ordered that her body, wrapped in white linen, be placed in the waters of the lagoon. He carried her body himself, followed by the grieving friends and family. When he placed the princess in the water, a miracle happened. The clear water changed color and became the same emerald green as the princess's beautiful eyes.

From morning to night, day after day, the Incan prince watched over his princess without ever taking his eyes off the water. Day after day he stayed, until one day he died.

That is why, from that moment until now, the lagoon is called the Lagoon of the Inca. And, Chileans say, that is also why, even today, the waters of the lagoon are such a deep emerald green.

A Sad Love Story

There is another Incan legend which explains why a small town in the north of Chile has the name *La Tirana* (The Tyrant).

It is said that there was once a beautiful Incan princess who led a band of brave Indian warriors in Tamarugal in the north of Chile. She was so famous for her beauty and her fierceness in killing Spaniards that she came to be called the Tyrant of Tamarugal.

One day, a young, handsome Portuguese miner named Vasco, who had wandered into the lands controlled by the princess, was taken prisoner and brought before her. According to the princess's own rules, the prisoner had to be killed. But as soon as the princess saw Vasco, she fell in love with him.

The princess, who was also a priestess, thought of a way to save Vasco's life. She told her warriors she would have to check her stars to see if he should die. That night, she declared he could not be killed until four full moons had passed.

The princess then took the prisoner into her own

living quarters. She forgot about her warriors and her battle with the Spaniards, and spent all her time with Vasco, making her soldiers angry and resentful.

The princess tried to convert Vasco to her religion, but instead he convinced her to convert to Christianity. The night before he was to die, they went to a clearing in the woods. Vasco baptized the princess and then, as they were about to be married, the princess's angry warriors rained arrows upon the two lovers, killing Vasco instantly. The princess was fatally wounded. Just before she died, the princess begged her warriors to bury them together and to put the cross with which she had been baptized on their grave.

Years later, a monk came upon the cross. When he heard the story, he built a temple on the spot and named it "Church of Our Lady of Carmen of La Tirana." Over the years, the place grew into a town, and a plaza was built in place of the temple. The princess is still remembered every July 16 in the Fiesta de La Tirana.

Goddess of the Sea

Chileans have created many stories which, at one time, were used to explain things the people could not understand. One of these is La Pincoya.

Chileans say that spirits live beneath the sunlight glinting on the sea. These spirits, called nymphs, are

Many Chileans earn their living from the sea, so legends about their struggle with the sea are common.

beautiful young women with long hair who ride through the waves on dolphins and sea horses. One of these sea nymphs is La Pincoya, the Goddess of the Sea.

La Pincoya is said to be a happy, laughing goddess with special powers over fish and shellfish. The wife of the god of fishermen, La Pincoya is considered a friend of the Mapuche Indians, and is said to have invented fishing nets to help them.

Sometimes, when the moon is full, La Pincoya is said to come out of the sea. With seaweed and algae wrapped around her for a dress, La Pincoya dances all night long on the sand by the edge of the sea. If a fisherman is lucky enough to see her, he can tell whether the next day's fishing will be good or bad. If she dances facing the sea, his nets will be full, but if she dances facing the mountains, he knows he and the other fishermen will return with empty nets.

Tuesday the Thirteenth

Hopes for the future and echoes of the past are shown in the sayings and superstitions popular in Chile. Some Chileans, especially in the countryside, are superstitious. While some may not really believe the superstitious sayings, they say them anyway.

Like Americans, Chileans say that if you break a mirror, you'll have seven years of bad luck. They also say that hearing an owl hoot is a sign that someone close to them will die soon.

Another superstition, which shows the difference in seasons between Chile and North America, is the belief that washing your hair in August will bring bad luck. This might seem strange if you think of August as a summer month. In Chile, though, August is in the middle of the winter. It is not hard to imagine that someone who uses an outdoor well or a river, as people who live in the country do, might catch a chill in the cold weather.

In Chile, the day to watch out for is not Friday the thirteenth—it is Tuesday the thirteenth! Some people say that it is bad luck to travel, get married, or do almost anything on Tuesday the thirteenth!

Some Chileans believe that unexplained noises and events are caused by spirits of dead people. For example, people say that spirits will come if a person works after midnight. One man who was digging outside after midnight claimed his shovel was suddenly pushed into the ground and became too heavy to lift. He believed the spirits were trying to tell him he had to stop working. Sometimes people light candles in the cemetery to ask for help from the spirits of dead people.

If someone is poor, then suddenly gets rich, Chileans might say that person made a pact, or agreement, with the devil. They say that if others don't pray when that person is about to die, the devil will take the soul.

The Early Bird Gets the Worm

Some Chilean sayings are similar to ones in English. One common saying is *"Del Dicho al hecho hay mucho trecho,"* or "From saying to doing there is quite a distance." In English, people say "Easier said than done."

Another saying is *"No par mucho madrugar amanece más temprano."* This means, "Getting up early doesn't make dawn come any sooner," which is similar to "A watched pot never boils."

One saying that probably comes from living near the ocean is *"Camarón que se duerme, so le lleva la corriente."* This means, "The shrimp that falls asleep gets carried away by the water." Chileans might say this about someone they think is lazy. Americans would say, "The early bird gets the worm."

Whether they believe in them or not, Chileans treasure their legends, sayings, and folktales. They are a valuable part of Chile's national heritage.

5. Good Times and Holiday Fun

Like people all over the world, Chileans like to get together with their friends and family, and enjoy celebrating holidays with special foods and things to do.

Monkey's Tail

New Year's is a favorite Chilean holiday. The celebrations begin around ten or eleven o'clock on the night of December 31, when families eat a late supper together. Adults often have a special drink made with coffee, milk, whiskey, sugar, cinnamon, and egg yolk called *"cola de mono,"* or "monkey's tail." Not many people know why it has the name "monkey's tail." Some say the name can be traced back to the 1500s when it was first made by Franciscan priests. Instead of whiskey, the priests used anise, a licorice-flavored liqueur that came in a bottle with a picture of a long-tailed monkey on the label. The priests mixed the drink and sold it in the anise bottles, so it came to be called "monkey's tail."

At midnight on New Year's Eve, Chileans hug and kiss each other, saying *"Buena suerte y que se cumplan todos sus deseos,"* which means "Good luck and may all your wishes come true." Some people stand on chairs while they hug each other because they believe that means they will get to travel a lot in the new year.

There are many beliefs about how to have good luck in the new year. Some people say that eating *lentejas*, or lentils, at midnight will bring good luck. Others believe if they make three wishes on New Year's Eve, those wishes will come true. Some Chileans believe they will have good luck if the first word they say after midnight is *conejo* (rabbit)!

After toasting the New Year at home with the family, young people often go to parties at each other's houses where they dance, sometimes until dawn. On New Year's Day people often go to the beach for a day out with family and friends.

Holy Week and Two Birthday Cakes

After New Year's, the next major holiday celebrated in Chile is *Semana Santa*, or Holy Week. During Semana Santa, Chileans celebrate Palm Sunday, Good Friday, and Easter Sunday. Chileans often go to church on these days.

On Palm Sunday, the churches give out palm branches. Chileans carry these palm branches in processions and then hang them on the walls of their houses. Some believe the branches will protect them and keep them safe.

On St. Peter's Day, some residents of Valparaíso gather to bless their fishing boats.

On Good Friday, there are processions around neighborhoods or towns in which people carry crosses in remembrance of Jesus. On Easter Sunday people go to mass. During the entire week classical music is played on the radio, and children are often warned not to whistle, yell, or say bad words.

Because so many Chileans are Catholic, saints' days are also important holidays. These are days named after a particular saint. Children often celebrate the saint's day with the same name as theirs. For example, a boy named Francisco or a girl named Francisca would celebrate his or her saint's day on October 4, the day of Saint Francis of Assisi. Boys and girls celebrate it like their birthday, with cake and perhaps a party with their friends. Then, on their birthday, they have another party and another cake!

One Potato, Two Potato

Some saints' days are celebrated by almost all Chileans. June 24, for example, which is *Día de San Juan*, or Saint John's Day, is celebrated in remembrance of John the Baptist. Juan and Juana are common names in Chile, so many families celebrate with a party that day. Some people also go to church.

There are many superstitions related to Saint John's Day. Some people write wishes on little pieces of paper and put them under their pillow. Later, they reach underneath it, and the one they pull out is the one that is supposed to come true. A Chilean girl might write the names of boys she knows on pieces of paper and put them under her bed. The one she pulls out is said to be the one she will marry.

Another custom is for unmarried girls to throw three potatoes under their bed—one peeled, one half-peeled, and one not peeled at all. After midnight, the girl reaches under her bed and pulls one out. If she takes the peeled one, she will be poor. If she pulls out the half-peeled one, she will be neither rich nor poor. If she pulls out the unpeeled potato, she will be rich.

Some Chileans say that if a person sees the flower of the fig tree on St. John's Day, she will have a lot of luck. If the person cuts the flower, she will be rich. But the flower has to be cut at midnight, without a light. There's one other thing that makes this hard to do—fig trees don't have flowers!

On saints' days, besides having parties or going to church, people fulfill *mandas*, or promises, made to a certain saint. For example, if a child is very sick, a mother and father might promise to do certain things if the saint heals their child. They might promise to light three packages of candles in church, or to dress their child only in brown or some other color for a month or even a year. Sometimes parents might promise to walk on their knees for a certain number of blocks. In areas where the roads are unpaved and full of stones, that can be a painful promise to keep.

Waving Flags and Handkerchiefs

The most important national holiday in Chile is *El 18 de Septiembre* (September 18), or Independence Day. It celebrates Chile's independence from Spain.

Red, white, and blue flags hang outside every home and in plazas and other public places. Families usually have a big lunch with typical Chilean foods such as *empanadas*, or meat pies, and then they go to the *fondas*. These are outdoor wooden booths covered with leafy branches and decorated with paper flags. People buy empanadas and wine or cider at the booths and have a picnic. While traditional Chilean music plays, people dance the *cueca*, the national dance.

The cueca is danced by a man and a woman. The man often wears a multi-colored poncho, flat-brimmed hat, and spurs, while the woman wears a swirling, full skirt. As the music plays and onlookers clap their hands, they twirl about each other, stamping their feet and waving handkerchiefs in the air.

Children's Day

One of the special events children look forward to is Children's Day. This comes in October and is part of a whole week schools devote to special celebrations such as Mother's Day, Teacher's Day, Flag Day, and Children's Day. Each day there are special performances, games, and competitions.

On Children's Day, there are all kinds of funny races at school. In one race, each child stands inside a sack and has to jump like a rabbit to reach the finish line. In another race, called *carrera de tres pies* (three-footed race), two children tie their left and right feet together and then have to hobble or hop to the finish line. There are also dance competitions where everyone takes part in typical Chilean dances such as the cueca and the *cumbia.*

Sometimes children also dress up in costumes on Children's Day, and prizes are given for the best costume. Once, in one class, a boy was so poor he had nothing for a costume, so his mother cut tree leaves and hung them on him. As he walked up to the stage, the leaves started falling off. The other children watching shouted, "It's autumn! It's autumn!" The boy won first prize for originality.

Feliz Navidad

Like children in other countries, Chilean children look forward to *Navidad,* or Christmas. Families decorate a Christmas tree or Christmas branches if they can't afford a tree. On December 24, families gather at about eleven o'clock in the evening for a festive meal. Children look forward to the special dessert, *pan de pascua,* a cake with fruit and nuts in it. Some families go to mass at midnight, then eat at about one o'clock in the morning!

After the meal, everyone opens his or her presents.

Chilean young people take part in a Nativity play during the Christmas season.

Children might get clothes or a bike, dolls, tops, or other toys. In poor families, parents often go without things so they can give their children chocolate or toys for Christmas. Everyone likes to make the people they love happy on this day.

Just a few days after Christmas, on December 28, is a holiday children especially enjoy. Called *El Día de los Inocentes* (Day of the Innocents), it is the same as April Fool's Day in the United States. On this day children play jokes on each other and on their parents. One practical joke is called *acortar las sábanas*—shortening the sheets. When no one is looking, they tuck the cover sheet around a bed in a certain way so that when the unlucky person tries to get into bed, his or her feet won't slide in!

All through the year Chileans look forward to their religious and national holidays. But even when there is no special holiday, Chileans like to get together to eat, dance, play the guitar, and enjoy themselves.

6. *Chileans at Home*

Most Chileans take great pride in their families and their homes. Even the poorest family will invite a guest to share a meal, saying, *"La casa es chica, pero el corazón es grande."* This means, "My house is small, but my heart is big."

Families in Chile are very close. Children usually live at home until they get married. Even after children are married, they often live with either the man or the woman's family; the family builds onto the same house so there is a place for everyone. Older people are especially respected and loved. Because they all live together, grandchildren see their *abuelito* (grandpa) and *abuelita* (grandma) all the time and are close to them.

In these big families, children always have someone to play with or talk to: their *hermanos* and *hermanas* (brothers and sisters), *primos* (cousins), *tíos* and *tías* (uncles and aunts), *abuelos* (grandparents), *madre* (mother), or *padre* (father). Often, friends visit, too. Grown-up friends of the family are called *tío* or *tía*, too, to show how close the family feels to them, even though they are not actually relatives.

The father is usually the head of the Chilean family. Though there have been some changes in the past few

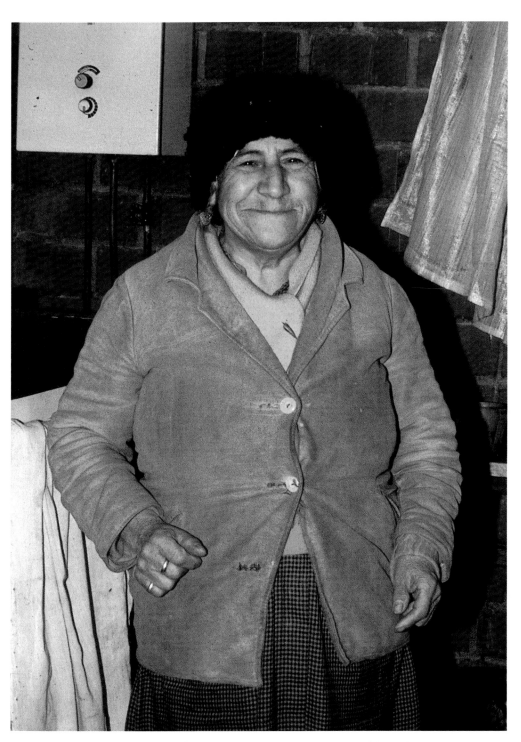

In Chile, older people are especially respected and loved.

years, most Chilean men believe in *machismo*. This means they feel the woman should stay home to cook, clean, and take care of the children. In spite of this, more Chilean women have begun to work outside the home, especially in poor families. If the father can't find work, the mother will help support the family.

Breakfast Talk

Mealtimes are an important part of family life. Parents and children eat together, telling each other about their day. Children talk about what they are doing in school and share jokes with their brothers and sisters. The family almost always eats at home. Though there are many restaurants in large cities, families usually don't go out to eat unless it is a very special occasion.

Chileans traditionally eat four meals a day. The first meal is *desayuno*, or breakfast, at around seven o'clock. The mother usually gets up first and prepares it, although some wealthy families have a maid who prepares the meals. Breakfast is a light meal of toast and milk for children, or toast and *café con leche* for adults. Café con leche is half a cup of hot coffee with half a cup of hot milk, sweetened with two or three teaspoons of sugar.

After breakfast the children go off to school. The father and the mother, if she works outside the home, might go to their jobs. If the mother stays home, she might clean the house, go shopping for food, and prepare *el almuerzo*, or lunch.

Lunch and Siesta

Lunch, the big meal of the day, is eaten at about two o'clock. In small towns and in some parts of big cities, businesses close from 1:00 to 3:00 P.M. so people can go home to have lunch with the whole family. Some businesses in the big cities have begun to stay open all day, but in most areas the children come home from school, and the parents come home from work to have lunch together.

In some families, two main dishes are served at lunch. The first dish might be salad with some of the seafood Chile is famous for, such as *erizos* (sea urchins) or *locos* (abalones). The second dish might be *cazuela de ave*, a thick soup with chicken, potatoes, carrots, rice, and parsley, or *porotos granados*, fresh beans cooked with corn, pumpkin, onion, and spices.

When Chileans eat dessert at lunch, it is usually a *manzana* (apple), *naranja* (orange), or some other fruit. Apples are eaten with a fork and knife, not by hand. The apple is first peeled (often in one long, connected spiral of apple peel), then sliced and eaten with a fork. *Flan*, a baked custard pudding, is another dessert children love. After lunch in the summertime, some people take a *siesta*, or nap, and then go back to work around 3:00 P.M. Children do their homework, play sports, or get together with their friends.

Tea Time

The third meal of the day is at 5:00 P.M. For *once* (OHN-say), or tea time, Chileans have coffee or tea, and toast with cheese or jam. Sometimes pastries are served, or, if it is a special occasion, a cake may be served. Children often invite friends to their house to have tea together.

Once actually means "eleven" in Spanish. There are two different stories about how tea time got its name. The first version claims that it is named after the time the British have their tea—11:00 in the morning. So even though in Chile tea time is at 5:00 in the afternoon, it is still called *eleven*.

The second version says that at tea time, men used to go into the kitchen or back room to have a sip of *aguardiente*, or whiskey, instead of tea. The men didn't want to say openly that they were drinking whiskey. Since the word *aguardiente* has eleven letters, they called tea time *once*.

After tea time, young people might go to a movie, play with their friends, read, watch television, or do more homework.

A woman shops for seafood at an outdoor market.

At about half past eight if there are young children, or later if the children are older, the family eats *la comida*, or supper. Supper is usually one main dish. It might be something like *bistec a lo pobre*, a steak topped with two fried eggs and served with french fries and fried onions. Although the name means "poor man's steak," some people say the name should be changed to *bistec a lo rico* ("rich man's steak") because poor Chileans cannot afford such a meal. Since supper is eaten late in the evening, children usually go to bed soon afterward.

The kinds of foods, and how many meals people eat, depend on their income. Poor families might have only one meal a day instead of four. They might have *porotos* (beans) every day, or only *pan* (bread) and tea because they can't afford a variety of foods.

National Foods

Like people everywhere, Chileans have special dishes that are national favorites. One is *empanadas*, pockets of dough filled with a mixture of chopped beef, onion, olives, raisins, and hard-boiled eggs, which are baked in the oven. These are a favorite on September 18—Chile's Independence Day—and other holidays. Empanadas can also be filled with cheese, then fried.

Humitas are another typical dish. These are made by grating fresh corn and mixing it into a paste with fried onions, basil, salt, and pepper. The mixture is then wrapped in corn husks and dropped into boiling water to cook. When they are done, the steaming little packages are unwrapped, and everyone has a treat.

Because fish and shellfish are so plentiful along Chile's coast, seafood dishes are common throughout Chile. One favorite is *paila marina*, a fish chowder.

Curanto is a dish made on Chiloé Island in the

south of Chile, and on Easter Island. It takes a whole day to make curanto. First a hole is dug in the ground and lined with stones. Fires are lit on top of the stones to make them very hot, then the wood and ashes are swept away. Great sacks of shellfish, pork, potatoes, vegetables, and bread dough are placed on top of the hot stones. The food sacks are covered with wet sacks, then grass and earth are piled into the hole to keep the heat inside. After several hours of steaming, the "oven" is opened, and the meal begins. In other parts of Chile, another version of curanto is prepared in large pots over a fire.

Some Chilean dishes, such as curanto, take a long time to prepare, but other Chilean recipes are easier to make. After you try the following recipes, you'll probably say, *"Es rico!"* ("It's delicious!")

Leche con Plátano (Banana Milk)

2 cups milk
1 sliced, ripe banana
1 teaspoon sugar (optional)

Put milk and banana in a blender. Blend until thoroughly mixed and foamy. Pour into a glass. Makes 2 servings.

Pastel de Papas (Potato Pie)

For mashed potatoes:
6 potatoes
2 cups cold water
a pinch of salt

For meat mixture:
1 pound ground beef
1 small onion, chopped
1 teaspoon garlic powder
1/2 teaspoon cumin
1 teaspoon parsley
1 teaspoon oregano
a dash of pepper
1 tablespoon flour dissolved in 1 tablespoon water
1 cup sliced black olives
2 eggs
1 cup raisins
1 tablespoon oil

Put the eggs in a small pot and cover with water.
Bring the water to a boil. Cover the pot and remove
from heat. Let the eggs sit in the water for about 20
minutes, then remove from water and cool in cold
water. Peel the shell from the eggs, then slice. Preheat your oven to 350°F.

Peel the potatoes and cut into eighths. Place these in a pot and cover with water (about 2 cups). Add the salt and bring to a boil. Cover and simmer at a low heat until a fork will pierce the potatoes easily. Pour off most of the water, and mash the potatoes with a potato masher or large fork until creamy. Add more water to the potatoes if necessary.

To make the meat mixture, first cook the chopped onion in oil until the onion is soft. Add the garlic powder, cumin, salt, parsley, oregano, and pepper. Pour this into a bowl. Next, brown the ground beef, then pour off the fat. Add the onion mixture to the meat and stir. Add the tablespoon of flour dissolved in water. Mix well.

Oil a loaf pan. Line the bottom of the pan with 1/2 of the mashed potatoes. Spread the meat mixture over the top of this, and sprinkle with the olives, raisins, and slices of hard-boiled egg. Cover this with the remaining mashed potatoes. Bake in a 350°F oven for 45 minutes. Serves 4.

Empanadas are a favorite Chilean dish. The following recipe is made with ground beef, but you can also use cheese.

Empanadas

Meat Filling:
1 pound ground beef
1/2 cup onions, chopped
8 black olives, chopped
1 teaspoon salt
1/4 teaspoon oregano

Pastry:
2-1/2 cups flour
1 egg yolk, beaten slightly
1/2 cup water
1/4 cup butter or margarine
1/2 teaspoon salt
1/2 teaspoon vinegar

To make the meat filling, brown the ground beef and onions in a frying pan. Drain off fat. Stir in the olives, salt, and oregano. Drain again by scooping mixture onto a paper towel. Set aside to cool.

To make the pastry, use your hands to mix together the flour, butter, egg yolk, and vinegar in a bowl. Stir the salt into the water and sprinkle it, a little at a time, over the flour mixture. Knead the dough by pressing it with your hands until it is smooth and stiff.

For each empanada, roll 1/4 cup of the dough into a circle with an 8-inch diameter. Place 1/2 cup of the meat filling on the circle, and fold it in half. Wet your fingers slightly and press the edges of the dough together. Poke each empanada several times with a toothpick to let the steam escape. Bake on a cookie sheet in a 400°F oven for 30 minutes.

For dessert, Chileans usually eat fresh fruit. But on special occasions, they might make a sweet, easy pudding called *flan*. If you'd like to serve flan with your meals, it's best to prepare it in advance.

Flan

11 heaping teaspoons of white sugar
4 eggs (one per person)
3 cups milk
1 teaspoon vanilla
1/4 teaspoon cinnamon

Preheat the oven to 400°F. Using oven mitts, heat a ring mold baking pan over a very low heat on top of the stove. (You might want to ask your parents for help with this part.)

After the baking pan has been heated, pour 7 heaping teaspoons of sugar into the pan. The sugar will melt and turn into dark brown caramel. As the sugar is melting, tilt the pan so it coats all sides of the pan evenly. Use a spoon to scoop up the melted sugar and spread it over the center of the pan, too. When the pan has been evenly coated with the melted sugar, set it aside.

In a bowl, beat together the eggs, milk, vanilla, cinnamon, and 4 teaspoons of sugar. Pour the mixture into the ring mold baking pan. (You will hear the sound of the caramel cracking as the cold mixture touches it.)

Place the ring mold in the oven and bake for one hour until the custard is no longer liquid. Cool, cover, and refrigerate until chilled. Serve straight from the pan, or turn upside down on a plate to remove from the mold. Serves 4.

7. *A Love for Learning*

Almost 94 percent of all Chileans know how to read and write; in fact, Chile has one of the highest literacy rates in Latin America.

Like children everywhere, most young people in Chile go to school every weekday. Instead of going to school from September to June, Chilean children attend classes from March to December, and summer vacation is in January and February.

Public Schools and Private Schools

There are both public and private schools in Chile. Some have all male or all female students, while others are coeducational. Many private schools are run by the Catholic church. There are also special language schools in which children learn all their subjects in French or English. This way, they develop very strong skills in the foreign language they choose.

Whether a student attends a public or private school, the school hours are the same. Children go to classes either from 8:15 A.M. to 1:15 P.M., or from 1:30 P.M. to 6:30 P.M. These split shifts are due to the lack of schools and teachers.

Every school day is divided into three periods of about one and one half hours each. The students do not move around from classroom to classroom for their different subjects; the teachers do. Between each period there is a ten-minute recess. Students go outside to play soccer, jump rope, or play other games with their friends.

Chilean students study many of the same subjects as students in the United States. They learn math, science, history and geography, technical education, music, art, and physical education. They also study Spanish grammar and literature. In addition, students can choose to study English, French, or German as a foreign language.

After school, children who attend morning classes go home for lunch with their families. Sometimes they return in the afternoon to play soccer or volleyball. A few schools offer choir or clubs for children interested in activities such as painting, literature, and computers.

Eight Years of School

In Chile, children are required to go to school for eight years, from age six to fourteen. They can then choose to go on to high school until they are eighteen years old, and to college after that if they can pass an entrance exam and afford the cost.

These students learn a variety of skills at school.

Until the age of eighteen, school is free, but students must buy their own supplies and uniforms. Boys wear navy blue pants, a white shirt, a blue tie, and a blue sweater. Girls wear a navy blue jumper or skirt, a white blouse, and white socks. Both girls and boys also wear a *delantal*, which looks like a scientist's laboratory coat, to protect their clothing. In some schools, the delantal is white, while in others it may have blue and white checks. At the end of the school year, everyone draws pictures and writes messages and poems on everyone else's delantal. By the time they have finished, the delantal looks like an autograph book!

Children who are very poor cannot afford notebooks, pencils, or special clothing for school, so they are not able to attend school. They might spend their day taking care of their younger brothers or sisters, or working at odd jobs. Some are forced to beg for money in the streets.

During the school year, Chilean students look forward to certain special events. May is the *mes del mar*, or month of the sea. During May, schoolchildren perform plays and work on other projects that teach them about the sea. In July, students have winter vacation for two weeks.

September is also a special month because Independence Day is celebrated on the eighteenth. During that month, students learn about Chilean national heroes, such as the first president, Bernardo O'Higgins. They write poems, plays, and essays about Chile's early years. September is also the time to take another vacation from school.

Exams and Universities

Most schools hold classes until the end of November and then give final exams. Each day the students take one or two different tests. Sometimes the exams are written, and sometimes they are oral. In an oral exam, the student stands before two or three teachers and is asked questions. The student is then graded on how well she knows the subject, and also on how well she expresses herself. Final exams usually make everyone nervous.

The most important exam a Chilean high school student takes is the *Prueba de Aptitud Académica* (Academic Aptitude Test), or P.A.A. This exam must be taken and passed by any student who wishes to go on to college. Students study very hard and worry a lot about the P.A.A. because their grade affects their future more than any other test they have taken until that time.

Some students who do well on the P.A.A. still might not be able to go to college because of the expense. For many years, university or college education in Chile was free. Today, because of changes in the educational system, only the very wealthy can afford to send their children to college.

Students stroll through the grounds at the Universidad Católica in Santiago.

The largest university in the country is the University of Chile. Founded almost 150 years ago, its main campus is in Santiago, but it also has campuses in Valparaíso, Antofagasta, and other cities throughout Chile. The Catholic University in Santiago and the University of Concepción are also very important universities.

College students must choose their particular field of study, such as law, engineering, or medicine, as soon as they enter college. This is different from the American system, where many students study liberal arts for two years and then decide on a major.

There are about eighteen universities throughout Chile, and their students are considered an important force in politics. Student organizations have worked for the return of a democratic government through peaceful demonstrations and other means.

Problems in Education

Many of Chile's schools today lack basic materials, such as books and maps. At times, teachers will buy books with their own money. Often, when teachers have only one copy of a book, they will read the information out loud so the class can copy it down. The students are then able to study from their notes as if from a book.

There is also a shortage of qualified teachers in Chile. Many teachers have been fired because of differences of opinion with school administrators and the country's government. Low wages also cause many teachers to leave the profession.

Before 1973, most Chileans were proud of their educational system and the fact that all Chileans had an equal opportunity to educate themselves. Also, while schools were funded by the government, they were not controlled by it. Today, the government decides what can and cannot be taught in both high schools and colleges. Subjects such as political science and the arts are no longer allowed at the universities, and many books are banned.

Students and teachers, however, attempt to restore the educational system to its former status. Recently, so many people protested against the head of the University of Chile that he was removed and replaced.

Despite the serious problems they face, Chileans still take pride in learning. They discuss poetry, literature, and politics, even if they have not been fortunate enough to attend college. It is their hope that their love for learning and desire for a better education will help them in their struggle for a better life.

8. *Free Time Fun*

From the mountains in the east to the western coast, Chileans take time out from work and school to ski, swim, sail, play games, watch television, go to movies, or meet with friends. Whatever the occasion, most Chileans join in with enthusiasm. Nowhere is this more evident than in the crowded stadiums where devoted fans gather to watch their country's most popular sport—soccer.

Soccer Fans

In the streets, on the beach, and at school, children kick soccer balls, bouncing them off their knees or heads to make a goal. Families watch their favorite teams in person or on television, and cheer for their favorite players.

Soccer is called *fútbol* in Spanish. American football is called *fútbol americano*, and is not played in Chile. Soccer is as popular as baseball and football are in the United States.

Colo Colo, Universidad Católica, and Universidad de Chile are some of the most popular teams in Chile. Players from each team are chosen each year for the national team, which goes on to play in the World Cup, the international soccer championship. As American children hope to play in the World Series or Super Bowl, Chilean children dream of one day playing in a championship game.

Skiing and Picnics

Skiing is also an important sport in Chile. The snow-covered Andes Mountains running the length of the country have made Chile world famous for its excellent skiing conditions. Since it is winter in Chile while it is summer in the northern hemisphere, skiers from all around the world come to ski in Chile from June to September. The most well known ski center is Portillo, about ninety miles (145 kilometers) northeast of Santiago, where the World Ski Championship was held in 1966. Famous skiers as well as people just learning to ski go to Portillo and the thirteen other ski centers throughout Chile.

Since skiing is an expensive sport, only well-to-do Chileans can afford to practice it. Many Chileans have never seen snow close up. Sometimes children take a field trip to the mountains so they can touch the snow and play in it. Everyone piles in a school bus and sings songs as they bounce along the narrow, rocky roads. When the bus gets as high up in the mountains as it can go, everyone gets out and climbs up to where the snow is.

Portillo, high in the Andes, is a popular ski resort.

Chile's long coastline makes water sports available almost everywhere in the country. People who can afford it go boating, water skiing, skin diving, and fishing, and many others go to the beach to swim or just lie in the sun. Families sometimes bring a picnic lunch and spend the whole day on the beach.

Other sports popular in Chile are basketball, volleyball, and tennis. Some young people enjoy throwing a frisbee around with friends.

Games, Games, Games

Many Chilean children like to play games. Sometimes they go to the corner arcade, called a "Flipper," to play video games, and sometimes they play games that anyone can play without money. A favorite game is *bolitas*, or marbles. Sometimes children will even play marbles in the street as they walk to school. They also like to play checkers. If a checkerboard and checkers aren't available, that doesn't stop them. They make their own checkerboard out of wood or cardboard and use bottlecaps for checkers.

Hopscotch and jumping rope are also popular. With just a piece of chalk, anyone can draw squares on the ground and play hopscotch, called *luche* in Chile. Also, an old piece of rope can be used to jump rope. Girls, especially, like to jump rope during recess at school.

For some games no materials at all are needed. *Piedra, Papel, Tijera* is like the game "rock, paper, scissors." Two people hold their hands behind their back and, at the same moment, put out one hand in the shape of either a scissors, knife, or rock. The scissors wins over the knife, the rock wins over the scissors, and the knife wins over the rock. If both players hold out the same sign, no one wins. Sometimes the person who loses pays the other one a certain number of bus tickets as a penalty.

For *Cielo, Luna, Mar* ("Sky, Moon, Sea"), all children need are three steps. One step is called the sky, another is the moon, and the last is the sea. Two people play. The first person calls out "Cielo!" and the other person has to jump to the step called *cielo*. The first person then calls out all the names one after the other, mixing them up. The person jumping has to jump on the right step without falling or he loses. After one person has a turn jumping, the two players switch places, and the other person jumps.

Chilean children also like to play with roller skates, balls, and kites. Some collect stickers, which they put in albums and trade with their friends. Pets are popular, too. The most common ones are dogs, cats, birds, and rabbits. Just like children in North America, Chileans enjoy having something soft and furry to cuddle and take care of!

Movies and Television

When they can, people in Chile like to go to the movies. They can see movies made in Chile and Europe, as well as the newest North American movies. The sound in foreign movies is dubbed so the actors and actresses appear to speak in Spanish rather than in English.

Like the movies, many TV programs shown in Chile are the same as those in the United States and Canada. But in Chile, Bill Cosby and He-Man speak Spanish! All the cartoons, police shows, soap operas, and other shows made in the United States are dubbed.

The most popular Chilean program is called *Sábados Gigantes*, or Giant Saturdays. During the show, which lasts almost seven hours—from 1:30 P.M. to 8:15 P.M. every Saturday—a live audience participates in contests and watches skits, interviews, and news reports. Don Francisco, the popular host of the show, has been on *Sábados Gigantes* for twenty-five years.

Some Chileans wish there were more shows made in Chile. They say that so many shows from another country make Chileans forget their own culture. They hope to be able to make more Chilean TV shows and movies in the future.

A young boy tries to untangle his kite from a tree.

The rodeo is one of the most popular sports in Chile.

Skill on Horseback

One entertainment that is very Chilean is the rodeo. Rodeos were first held in Chile more than four hundred years ago. In the beginning, the rodeo was organized to round up and sort out cattle so they could be counted and branded. As the years went by, rodeos became contests in which the huaso displayed his skill herding cattle.

Today the rodeo takes place in a semi-circular ring called a *medialuna*. Two horsemen work together to chase a bull around the ring and corner him against a specially marked area of the railing. They win points depending on how fast they are and how well they stop the bull against the fence.

Spectators sit around the ring, cheering the horsemen. Nearby, booths are set up where people can buy empanadas and other types of food, dance, and listen to folk music.

There are more than two hundred rodeo clubs throughout Chile where thousands of two-man teams compete to see who will go to the National Rodeo Championship held every March in Rancagua, a city just south of Santiago. Children dream of the day when they, too, will be so good on horseback that they win honors at the rodeo.

When summer comes, in January and February,

families go to the beach or the mountains if they can. In the mountains they might go horseback riding, swim in ponds, and play with friends. Some families rent or own a summer home where they go when they take a vacation.

With its varied landscape and fine weather, Chile is a good place to enjoy an assortment of sports, games, and activities. Many Chileans have found that it doesn't take a lot of money to have fun. Whether they are playing guitars and singing with a group of friends, or having a cup of coffee with family members, Chileans welcome the chance for free time fun and entertainment.

9. Chileans in the United States

Chileans are dedicated to their country, and hardly ever choose to leave it. Only very difficult situations have caused large numbers of them to say good-bye to their families, the beautiful mountains, and the sea.

Gold Fever

The first group of Chileans to come to the United States was attracted by stories of the Gold Rush in 1848. Thousands of Chileans sailed to California that year to join the frantic search for gold. They were not welcomed by the American miners, however, who wanted to keep the gold for themselves. The Foreign Miners' Tax, passed in 1850, required foreigners to pay twenty dollars a month for a license to look for gold. Disappointed, many Chileans and other Latin Americans stopped going to California to look for gold.

More than one hundred years later, in the 1960s, another group of Chileans came to the United States in search of better jobs and the opportunity to improve their lives. Many of these Chileans became American citizens. Today, they speak English to their children and have adopted the American way of life.

Political Refugees

Since the military coup in 1973, thousands more Chileans have come to the United States. They came not to look for better jobs, but because they felt they were in danger from General Pinochet's military government. These people are called political refugees because they are looking for a refuge, or a safe place, from a political situation that they think threatens their lives in their own country.

In all, one out of every ten Chileans left Chile as a result of the coup—almost 1 million people. Many went to Europe, Canada, Venezuela, and other parts of Latin America, as well as the United States.

Some Chilean refugees found it hard to adjust to life in the United States. One of the biggest problems they faced was the language. Immigrants who could not speak English found themselves unable to communicate with the people around them. They solved this problem by going to classes to learn to speak, read, and write in English.

Another problem faced by the Chilean refugees was finding a job. Chileans who could not speak English, or whose degrees and licenses were not recognized in the United States, found themselves working in unskilled jobs. Some of these people had been doctors, professors, or other kinds of professionals before they left their country. Through hard work and dedication, though, many have begun to reenter their former professions.

In a Strange Land

Chileans in the United States are grateful for the opportunity to come here, and for the many material things that are available. But unlike many immigrants to the United States, some Chilean refugees did not want to leave their country. They came here because of the political situation in Chile. Although these Chileans try to accept their new life in the United States, they hope to return to their homeland some day. They miss their friends and family members who are still in Chile, and they miss their old way of life.

Another thing Chileans miss is their language—Spanish. Chileans who live in large cities, such as Los Angeles and New York City, can speak with other Chileans and people from other parts of Latin America. But in some places, there aren't large numbers of Spanish-speaking people. Many families speak their native language at home so their children will grow up knowing it. Sometimes the children, who hardly remember Chile or were never there, prefer to speak English.

Chileans in the United States try to preserve their language, traditional foods, and celebrations. Some

A mural outside of La Peña's offices shows a variety of arts important to Chileans.

live in communities where they are the only Chileans, and they find it hard to maintain their customs. Others live near other Chilean families, and they get together to celebrate special holidays. They cook empanadas, play Chilean music, and dance. A cultural center in Berkeley, California, called *La Peña*, organizes Chilean musical events and keeps people informed about what is going on in Chile. Some Chilean families have organized soccer teams and continue to play their national sport.

Being together helps keep alive their traditions and ways of life.

Chileans try to preserve their country's customs in a variety of ways. Some sell Chilean handicrafts in the United States, sending the money they earn back to Chile so the people who make them can afford to feed their families. Chileans tell the story of the crafts when they sell them, sharing their love for their country and describing what it is like to live there.

In 1988 the Chilean government announced that some Chileans who had been forbidden to return to Chile could go back. Many did return, eager to vote in the October 1988 election. Other Chileans, however, chose to remain in the United States. For some families that have been here for many years, the United States has become their home. Although they miss Chile, they have created a new life here, and are happy with the choices they have made.

Chilean Influences

Chileans have been contributing to American life and culture since they first began arriving in large numbers in the 1800s. Claudio Arrau is a Chilean pianist who lives in New York City and is well known around the world. He was born in 1903 in Chillán, a small town just north of Concepción. His mother was a

Claudio Arrau.

piano teacher, and his father, who died when Claudio was only a year old, was an optometrist.

At the age of five, Arrau was recognized as a musical genius, and at the age of six he played the piano for the president of Chile. With the support of the Chilean government, he was sent to study in Germany. He lived there for some years, teaching and giving concerts around the world. In 1941, he moved to New York City and has lived there ever since.

Now nearly ninety years old, Claudio Arrau is recognized as one of the greatest pianists ever to play Beethoven. He has made many records and still gives concerts.

Speaking Out for Freedom

Isabel Margarita Letelier, a Chilean who lives in Washington, D.C., is one of the best-known Chileans in the United States. She was born in Santiago, where her father was a business executive and her mother a teacher and actress. Isabel Letelier has four sons and has lived in the United States for much of the past thirty years.

Isabel Letelier first came to the United States in 1960 with her husband Orlando, who later became Chile's ambassador to the United States. He was also a foreign minister and minister of defense in Salvador Allende's government.

Isabel Letelier.

After the military coup in 1973, Orlando was arrested and taken to a concentration camp on cold, windy Dawson Island in southern Chile. For a year, he and other former officials of Allende's government were starved, frozen, and forced to haul and break rocks. Isabel organized a movement to free him from prison, which finally resulted in his release and exile to Venezuela. Soon afterward, the Letelier family moved to Washington, D.C.

In September 1976, Orlando Letelier was killed in Washington, D.C., along with an American co-worker, Ronni Karpen Moffitt, when a bomb blew up his car. Since that time, Isabel Letelier has worked to identify and bring to trial her husband's murderers.

After an investigation and trial, two Cuban exiles and an American working for the Chilean secret police were convicted of the murders. The head of Chile's secret police and two other secret police officials were also found to be involved, but the Chilean government refused to send them to the United States to stand trial. The case is still open, with continuing investigations and attempts to punish those responsible for the assassination.

Today Isabel Letelier works at the Institute for Policy Studies in Washington, D.C., where she is in charge of the Human Rights Project and Third World Women's Project.

Even though they live far away from their native land, Chileans in the United States are still drawn to the mountains, sea, and traditions of their country.

A Love for the Land

Most Chileans are eager to take advantage of the opportunities they have found in the United States. Yet whether they live here or in Chile, Chileans share a deep love for their country. The beautiful landscapes and the warmth and friendliness of the people make it a place to remember and treasure always.

Appendix

Chilean Consulates in the United States and Canada

The Chilean consulates in the United States and Canada offer information to people wishing to learn more about Chile. For information and resource materials, contact the embassy or consulate nearest you.

U.S. Consulates and Embassy

Chicago, Illinois
  Consulate General of Chile
  333 North Michigan Avenue
  Seventh Floor
  Chicago, Illinois 60601
  Phone (312) 726-7097

Houston, Texas
  Consulate General of Chile
  Texas Commerce Towers
  1360 Post Oak Boulevard
  Houston, Texas 77056
  Phone (713) 621-5853

Los Angeles, California
  Consulate General of Chile
  510 West Sixth Street
  Suite 1204
  Los Angeles, California 90014
  Phone (213) 624-6357

Miami, Florida
  Consulate General of Chile
  25 Southeast Second Avenue
  Suite 801
  Miami, Florida 33131
  Phone (305) 373-8623

New York, New York
  Consulate General of Chile
  866 United Nations Plaza
  Suite 302
  New York, New York 10017
  Phone (212) 980-3366

Philadelphia, Pennsylvania
  Consulate General of Chile
  Public Ledger Building
  Sixth and Chestnut streets
  Philadelphia, Pennsylvania 19106
  Phone (215) 829-9520

San Francisco, California
  Consulate General of Chile
  870 Market Street
  Suite 1062
  San Francisco, California 94102
  Phone (415) 982-7662

Washington, D.C.
  Chilean Embassy
  1732 Massachusetts Avenue, N.W.
  Washington, D.C. 20036
  Phone (202) 785-1746

118

Canadian Consulates and Embassy

Montreal, Quebec
Consulate General of Chile
1010 Saint Catherine Street West
Montreal, Quebec H3B 3R3
Phone (514) 861-8006

Ottawa, Ontario
Chilean Embassy
56 Sparks Street
Suite 801
Ottawa, Ontario K1P 5A9
Phone (613) 235-4402
(613) 235-9940

Toronto, Ontario
Consulate General of Chile
330 Bay Street
Room 1308
Toronto, Ontario M5H 2S8
Phone (416) 366-9570

Vancouver, British Columbia
Consulate General of Chile
1130 West Pender Street
Vancouver, British Columbia
V6E 4A4
Phone (604) 689-8101

Glossary

abuelita (ah·bway·LEE·tah)—grandma

abuelito (ah·bway·LEE·toh)—grandpa

abuelos (ah·BWAY·lohs)—grandparents

acortar las sábanas (ah·kawr·TAHR lahs SAH·bah·nahs)—"shortening the sheets"; a joke played on "Día de los Inocentes"

aguardiente (ah·gwahr·dee·EHN·tay)—whiskey

allanamiento (ah·YAHN·ah·mee·EHN·toh)—a raid by soldiers and police

almuerzo (ahl·MWAIR·soh)—lunch

arpilleras (ahr·pee·YAIR·ahs)—wall hangings made from bits of cloth sewn in the shape of a picture

bistec a lo pobre (bee·STAYK ah loh POH·bray)—"poor man's steak"; steak with two fried eggs on top, french fries, and fried onions

bolitas (boh·LEE·tahs)—marbles

buenos días (BWAY·noh THEE·ah)—good morning

café con leche (kah·FAY kohn LAY·chay)—"coffee with milk"; a drink made with hot coffee, sugar, and hot milk

cafetera (kah·fay·TAIR·ah)—a coffeepot

callampas (kah·YAHM·pahs)—"mushrooms"; very poor neighborhoods

carrera de tres pies (kah·RAIR·ah day TRAYS pee·AYS)—three-footed race

cazuela de ave (kah·SWAY·lah day AH·vay)—thick chicken soup

chao (CHOW)—good-bye

charango (chah·RAHNG·oh)—string instrument made from an armadillo shell

Cielo, Luna, Mar (see·AY·loh, LOO·nah, MAHR)—"Sky, Moon, Sea"; a jumping game

cola de mono (KOH·lah day MOH·noh)—"monkey's tail"; a New Year's drink made of coffee, milk, whiskey, sugar, cinnamon, and egg yolk

comida (koh·MEE·thah)—supper

conejo (koh·NAY·hoh)—rabbit

conquistadores (kohn·kees·tah·DAWR·ays)—"conquerors"; Spanish soldiers who came to Latin America in the 1500s and conquered the Indians

cueca (KWAY·kah)—the national dance of Chile

cuidado (kwee·THAH·oh)—be careful

cumbia (KOOM·bee·ah)—a dance popular in Chile

curanto (koo·RAHN·toh)—a dish made in Chile of fish, shellfish, pork, and vegetables, baked in a hole in the earth

delantal (day·lahn·TAHL)—apron or lab coat worn over school clothes to keep them clean

desayuno (day·sah·YOO·noh)—breakfast

empanadas (ehm·pah·NAH·thahs)—baked pockets of dough filled with chopped beef, onions, olives, raisins, and hard-boiled eggs; a Chilean national dish

erizos (ay·REE·sohs)—sea urchins

"es rico" (AYS REE·koh)—"it's delicious"

flan (FLAHN)—baked custard pudding eaten as a dessert

fondas (FOHN·dahs)—wooden booths covered with leafy branches and decorated with paper flags

fundos (FOON·dohs)—large estates or ranches

fútbol (FOOT·bohl)—soccer

hermanas (air·MAH·nahs)—sisters

hermanos (air·MAH·nohs)—brothers

"hola, ¿qué hubo?" (OH·lah, KYOO·boh)—"Hi, how are you?"

huaso (WAH·so)—Chilean cowboy

humitas (oo·MEE·tahs)—grated corn, onions, and spices wrapped in corn husks and boiled

inquilinos (een·kee·LEE·nohs)—farm workers on large estates

La Laguna del Inca (lah lah·GOO·nah dehl EEN·kah)—"Lagoon of the Inca"; a lagoon near Portillo

leche con plátano (LAY·chay KOHN PLAH·tah·noh)—a drink made of cold milk blended with bananas

lentejas (lehn·TAY·hahs)—lentils

locos (LOH·kohs)—abalones, a kind of shellfish

luche (LOO·chay)—hopscotch

machismo (mah·CHEES·moh)—a sense of masculine pride; the belief that a man should be the head of the family

madre (MAH·dray)—mother

mandas (MAHN·dahs)—promises made to a saint in exchange for help

manzana (mahn·SAH·nah)—apple

mar (MAHR)—the sea

medialuna (MAY·thee·ah·LOO·nah)—"half moon"; a semi-circular ring where rodeos take place

mestizo (mehs·TEE·soh)—a person of Spanish and Indian ancestry

naranja (nah·RAHN·hah)—orange

Navidad (nah·vee·THAHTH)—Christmas

olla común (OH·yah koh·MOON)—community cooking pot in which poor people share their food with each other

once (OHN·say)—"eleven"; tea time

padre (PAH·dray)—father

palafitos (pah·lah·FEE·tohs)—fishing villages with houses on stilts

pan (PAHN)—bread

pan de pascua (PAHN day PAHS·kwah)—fruitcake eaten at Christmas time

Piedra, Papel, Tijera (pee·AY·drah, pah·PEHL, tee·HAY·rah)—a game similar to "rock, paper, scissors"

La Pincoya (lah peen·KOY·yah)—a sea nymph believed to be the goddess of the sea

poblaciones (POH·blah·see·OHN·ays)—very poor neighborhoods

porotos granados (poh·ROH·tohs grah·NAH·thos)—fresh beans cooked with corn, pumpkin, onion, and spices

primos (PREE·mos)—cousins

Prueba de Aptitud Académica (proo·AY·bah day ahp·tee·TOOD ah·cah·DAY·mee·kah)—Academic Aptitude Test; an exam required to get into college

quena (KAY·nah)—small bamboo flute

siesta (see·EHS·tah)—a nap

Tierra del Fuego (tee·AIR·rah dehl FWAY·goh)—"land of fire"; part of southern Chile

tía (TEE·ah)—aunt

tío (TEE·oh)—uncle

Unidad Popular (oo·nee·THAHTH poh·poo·LAHR)—Popular Unity political party headed by Salvador Allende

Selected Bibliography

Agosin, Marjorie. *Scraps of Life: Chilean Arpilleras.* Trenton: The Red Sea Press, 1987.

Boraiko, Allen A. "Acts of Faith in Chile." *National Geographic*, July 1988, pp. 54-85.

Chavkin, Samuel. *Storm Over Chile: The Junta Under Siege.* Westport: Lawrence Hill and Co., 1985.

Chile Information Network. *ChiliNet* 8. November 1988.

Hauser, Thomas. *Missing.* New York: Avon, 1978.

Hintz, Martin. *Chile: Enchantment of the World.* Chicago: Childrens Press, 1985.

Jara, Joan. *An Unfinished Song: The Life of Víctor Jara.* New York: Ticknor & Fields, 1984.

Neruda, Pablo. *Memoirs.* New York: Farrar, Straus and Giroux, 1977.

Samalgaski, Alan. *Chile and Easter Island, a Travel Survival Kit.* Berkeley: Lonely Planet Publications, 1987.

Index

About the Author

During her research for *Chile: Land of Poets and Patriots*, Irene Flum Galvin drew from her experiences as an exchange student at the University of Concepción in Chile, as well as from those of her many Chilean friends. In writing this book, the author hopes to "make Chile come alive for children so  they know it is a real place with real people who hope and dream and care about life as they do."

Ms. Galvin's educational background includes a Bachelor's degree in Spanish and French from the State University of New York at Binghamton, and a Master's degree in education from Harvard University. She is currently the vice president of a marketing communications firm in Rochester, New York, where she lives with her husband and two children.